The Bad Seed

— *Stride* —

This collection is dedicated to Aideen Cusack and Crow. May you be (re)filled with the spirit, energy & vision we shared, back in 1984. Also to Maurice Cox, a true teacher; and Rebecca Wright, a true daughter.

Love & respect to my true family: you know who you are!

THE BAD SEED
Dee Rimbaud

THE BAD SEED
First edition 1998
© Dee Rimbaud

ISBN 1 900152 20 7

Cover drawing by Dee Rimbaud
Cover design by Neil Annat

Acknowledgements
*Abraxas, Ambit, Axiom, Borderlines, Bradford Poetry Quarterly,
Braquemard, Chronicles Of Disaster, Dada Dance, Doors,
Headlock, Helicon, Magazing, Martin Holroyd's Poetry Monthly,
Moonstone, Orbis, Ramraid Extraordinaire, Sepia, Sol, Stride,
Terrible Work, Little Red Book, TOPS, Understanding.*

Published by
Stride Publications
11 Sylvan Road, Exeter
Devon EX4 6EW

with the assistance of
the Ralph Lewis Award
at the University of Sussex

CONTENTS

CANDY

1.

In the dripping heart, a dull descant beats:
The ways of ends and means, cross-hatched,
Concrete, latticed, strapped and lashed,
The fish hook in arterial flesh, wrenched,
Thrust, the stretched gut, taut, held fast,
Quivering a five tone drone, a blue chord,
A negroid ache
Under the rock's weight, the chain gang
Flange, tight tied,
A cruciform guttered scream:
This is the way of ends and means;
This here night that undermines day.

2.

In the dripping heart, an arc of dark fire,
The penumbra encircling the sun, my dreams
Infected,
Black stallions stampeding,
Trampling down this human flesh,
Thundering blood over emerald grass:
Their fearsome masculine fury,
Trumpetting Jericho, issuing out
Seven plagues, the seven vengeances
Of a jealous God;
Each an Angel, a history,
A hysterectomy;
And I am aborted,
Dissolved in entropy,
The dark juice of the dark mother –
She tears the hymen from my eyes.
Durga, Kali Ma, Candy:
In the beginning
You will be the end of me.

3.

In delirium tremens and sinking,
A precognition of my fate:
And still I wait
And still I wait,
The tight fist of viscera
The hand that hammers
Blunted nails
(a heart, after all
is only worth its palpitations)
And still I wait;
Supine, submissive,
Stomach clenched,
Arms outstretched.

See the leeched labia
Indenting these palms, Candy?
They are waiting
Only for your giving:
And this mouth?
It is parched and bleeding,
Ever ready to receive
The spat fragments
Of your bad seed.

1:The Bad Seed

THE BAD SEED

I.

This one is sunset red, rich as womb blood,
Thick as flesh:
It tastes of fire and sex
And finger probes the hollow folds
Of dormant rotten mass
While eggshell strips are slowly ripped
With tainted talons and Godless taunts.

The blue is sharp, neon, etheric,
Cauterising the eyes,
A topography of dilapidated sky:
It shrivels the soul
In static strata –
The stark vastness
Of its wide open
Restless space,
A question mark?

And this fibre of daffadown yellow:
It grips and scorches
The sleeping heart
With cruel springtime
Flick knife twists –
A cabbage moth
On wings of vacant hope.

These strands of primal colour
Weaving through light and dark
Spirals of sunken spectrum:
A loom of illumination;
Its cloth,
A spectral aquarelle
Of phosphorescent wash,
An edgeless sfumato rainbow;
Dazzling,
But ever deceptive
To the finger's tentative touch.

See this pink one?
It promises purification:
The cold calm recollection
Of selfless, soul-embracing love,
But do not listen to its lies –
For like a siren sat on coral rocks
Its song will surely tempt you
To the massive heaving shoreline
And dash your spirit to dust.

And this mossy Kerry green:
A corrosive mist which dimly caresses
The steely harp's catgut strings,
Ringing out a saline tune
Which rusts the bridge
Which spans the years
From battered birth to wistful grave.

And all these colours, a blurred contusion
And all the polychromatic confusion
From mother of pearl to brown and grey,
A myriad hues of every shade:
From sable strokes on sacking cloth
And pigment smears of clotted oil,
The sheeted mirror of wants and needs;
A lust for life and trust in death,
A karmic cheque of thoughts and deeds,
These rainbow ribbons which steal the breath.

2.

The web is flexible, but tightly spun,
Allowing the illusion of movement
Whilst holding you fast.
There is the smell of cordite and sweat
And a vague hint of threat,
But nothing tangible,
Nothing you can grasp.
(And anyway, your hands are tied.)

You dance in the shaman's shadow,
A whirling dervish,
Trailing ribbons in your wake,
In acid arcs of burning colour.
You are dancing in a dreamscape,
A shifting topography
Of ruined cities, deserts
And empty highways.
There is a vague hint of holocaust,
But nothing tangible.
(And anyway, it's always summer now
In your dreams.)

Imagine then, the book of the dead
Lying unread
On your bedside table.
Imagine the smells of sex and sweat,
The upturned cup of blood,
The vomit pile
Of black bile flowers.

Now, enter the actor, stage left:
A cascade of black narcissi
Clasped to his breast.
He kisses them in the half light
With fat petulant lips
All a-pouting;
And plucks them from their stems
With fickle finger tips
As his audience watches, delighted,
In suspense:
Waiting for something to snap.

And in the unlit back alley
Where the wind whips up
The weekend's detritus
A primal drama is re-enacted:
Hunter and quarry
Pirouette
A pornographic hieroglyph —

Iconoclastic,
In the stillness of the night.

And then you're back in this city room
With the rain falling all over the blankets
And her sobbing beside you,
A broken doll
In your thick arms,
A thesaurus of platitudes
Spilling from your tongue,
And the echo of a scream
Ringing round your ears.

Then the contractions come on,
Tight
And tighter still:
There's klaxons and sirens and bells;
And ribbons, all pretty coloured,
Blowing about like a bloody jamboree.

3.

He was naked on the motorway, running away:
Tattered fetters trailing from his wrists;
The sweat dribbling in his eyes,
Burning.
He was running blind:
His head, a blur
Of cathode radiation.

It was a particularly twisted sadism
That caused them to inflict upon him
The hollow brands and blandishments
Peculiar to their station.
"Cruel to be kind
And kind to be cruel," they said,
Whilst rubbing together
Their fat glutinous hands
And secreting saliva
From involuntary glands.

And all the while inside,
Deep inside,
The small boy
Who's trying to hide:
The small boy
They cannot touch
Who misses his mummy
Very much.

And through the filthy smog of time
With all its chaos and its grime
You want to reach and grab the light
And assure the boy it'll be alright.

But there's no reaching back now:
The turnpike here
Only twists one way
And the turnpike keeper
Must be paid.

You know those celluloid strips
Lodged in your brain?
They cannot be edited:
Only played
Again and again and again.

4.

They made him take the ribbons in his hands
And tie them up in patterns and proportions
With numbers and common denominations
In fractious factions
Associated with corporations
Where mumbo jumbo preachers preached:
"Each according to his station"
And pointing pedants each repeated
A list of rules and regulations
While tangents curved their measured arcs
Of quadratic inequation
(and this indeed they deigned to call
a 'comprehensive' education).

They said it was good for him, this.
They said it was good, but he never heard.
He just went right on crying
On and on about the dead bird:
The dead bird on the splattered tarmac,
All red blood and neon green.

So they tied him up and made him smile
And stuffed his head with cotton wool
And filled him up unto the brim
With whisky, sex and gold.
They said that it was good for him,
Good for him to be a man:
So he smiled & drank & fucked & fought
And placed a mask upon his face.

And when at last he was undone
They let him go upon his way,
Past the turnpike and the toll
Then over the hills and far away.

5.

He watched,
In shock,
The black bird
Spiral and fall
And crash,
Crash black
Into the tarmac:
A slash of black
Thru' a sky
Of silver and neon.

Sweet bird of death,
Sweet bird
In a sick green world.

He stooped over
And watched:
So unable to touch.

Charcoal thing,
So little
In its broken wings
With its broken eyes
And broken beak.

Charcoal
In the charnel soil:
Falling and flailing
In short sharp gasps
Of the nervous end.

6.

These brackish waters
Do not slake the thirst,
Nor put out
The acid fires
That burn the holes within.

7.

This bird is shallow shadow:
A grey echo, receding,
Retreating into grey dawn —
Its bleached bones, broken;
The gawping beak,
Singing no song.

8.

This seed has grown within:
A barren twisted tree;
Its roots thrust into acrid soil;
Its branches flocked
With winged cadavers
Who fuck and fight
And eat and shit
Under awnings

Of rotten blossom
And disappointed fruit.

9.

The girl with the sugarsweet smile
Is no longer sweet or smiling:
Her face is copper green,
Scrubbed clean
Of all expression;
And any lingering trace of secretion
Has neatly been showered away.

The only tangible impression
Of any emotion
Is seen in the trembling of hands;
And these you imagine
Viciously pulling
Tighter and tighter,
The ribbons around your brain.

10.

In the pissing river,
Drinking the dust
Into your lungs:
Penitent,
Arched
And straining;
And all the while
The pissing river
Raining
Raining
Raining.

11.

Upon the terracotta ribbon strand
The Angel entreats him,

Silently pleading:
"Behold the lamb of God!"

The lamb stares blindly out
From bleeding inward eye,
Crying aloud: "My God, My God,
Why didst Thou deceive me?"

Oil black crow
Sweeps a parabola arc,
Crashing black
Into the tarmac.

The motorway is empty, eerie:
He treads the tarmac wordlessly,
Ether & blood & ice
Pumping to the rhythm of the night.

The Angel, all-knowing,
But elusive,
Gives a knowing look:
Alludes to the good seed,
Buried safe
Behind the looking glass.

Crumpled by gravity,
He peers gravely
Into the glass:
A pool of fool's gold.

The crow,
Black and majestic,
Laughs;
And in one swift
Mercurial leap,
Impales the lamb
Upon his beak.

12.

Stranded on the central reservation,
Soaked in oily spindrift,
With the seagulls calling:
Black waves crash
Upon shifting sands
And the sun beats down,
Relentless.

Along the strand,
Shimmering in heat haze,
An Angel approaches,
Beckoning.

Then she's gone:
Just the motorway remaining;
And in the depths of sky,
No stars,
No fire –
Only the pissing river,
Raining
Raining
Raining.

13.

Her eyes are red and dry:
The war rages
In the dark corners
Of her head.

Mirrors and windows are sheeted:
Shadowy figures mourn
The passing
Of the dead.

14.

He kisses her hair
And says: "there there",
But his mind is elsewhere.

He blows an indifferent whisper
Into the depths of her ear
And little shivers run thru' her,
Like the shivering of waves
On a cold blue sea.

Her eyes are pools:
Her mouth, a river;
Her body, an ocean.
He treads her restless shoreline,
Uneasily naked,
A starfish grasped
In his soft wet hand.

Fumble fingered,
He strokes it;
And filaments of dust
Detach and fall,
Feathery as spindrift.

15.

She talks about her father;
And the dislocation
In the faraway spaces
Behind his eyes.
Her voice is soft,
Almost sobbing:
It murmurs like the riptide.

Her father had strange eyes:
He was a stranger
From a faraway place.

She touches her breast,
Cries a broken doll cry,
"Papa, papa."
Her eyes glaze,
Skin flowers red:
"Love me, love me," she says.

Her body thrashes beneath him:
An angry ocean,
Swollen
And torn open.

16.
They fuck on the motorway:
The crows go wild
And fly away.

She is cool, blue eyed:
Slow as a river in floodtide.

The process is sad and unending:
A funeral procession
Thru' childhood streets;
Past crumbling buildings
And open closemouths
Where lovers trade
Darkling kisses,
Shaky and bursting.

His eyes are ashes,
His lips dry:
The birds are scattered;
A flurry of black wings
Clattering
Against a rusted metal sky.

Loneliness creeps upon him,
Wraps her tarry arms
Around his broken frame
And drags him further in.

17.

She whispers her panic into his ears:
Endless channels and passages
Into empty space.
He is dreaming in empty space.

They fuck
In blind, groping fury,
Clinging together:
They come together
And come apart.

Her tears are a dream in empty space.
The song is sung
And everything is done and undone.

They hold onto each other:
They hold on for dear life.

2: Rip Tide

HOME IS WHERE THE HARPIC IS

Abraxas is curled up in the corner,
Sniggering idiot child,
Dreamer of uncertain destinies.

He weaves a tappist finger of smiles,
Twists pretty
And traps the shiny thread
In echoes of kitchen sinking.

Here then is the unfolding:
The dissolution of subtext
And subterfuge;
A spindrift riptide
Dragging you ever under.

A DIET OF WORMS

Twists pretty face fine featured,
Walks on fragrant heels,
Bubbles wine & laughter
All over the place;
And coy depreciating smiles
To all the boys...
I strangle her in my sleep.
Heavy dreams & wired perception,
In heat,
Helter skeltered
Thru' the bedclothes
And touched her ivory hands
And (she wasn't there, never there)
Cried out
For the warm breath of light,
Light in the dark,
Mother mother,
And wished sweet sleep to overcome,
To dowse with clear water
The flame that fires this frenzy
And twist the knot untwisted
From the brow
Of head
Of dead dead
Of red raw screaming,
Thrashing
In the naked sweat,
Arms and limbs and sex,
Bursting,
Thirsting
For the touch of a cold clean hand,
Mother mother,
Pulling back the blankets,
Squirming in the wet raw
Sticky stuff.

•

Enough enough!
I smash silver fingers
For mirrors of light,
Scrape cinder night
From the pit:
Admit defeat,
Let me sleep
Let me sleep
Let me sleep.

•

Joe Silver talks rhyme
& nonsense, whisky
& deliverance.
He wakes in the city
With crap on his hands
And stares in the mirror
Oh mother!
I drive thru' the forest,
Thru' shadows of
Blackness of night,
For a fuck in penitence,
In a black hearth,
In a black soul.

•

Whisky & wine smelling
Mother lover,
She would take me
To her jasmine bed
And smother me
In her milky limbs.

•

Alone, unresolved, fevered,
I burst in symphony,
Black & white,
Crawling thru' the bushes

With no name,
With the starling's cry
In the snake awakening asphalt
Cracked & sunken city.

MOTORWAY GHOST

Monosynthesis, this raw jazz in sherbert fizzed arteries
Of motorway madness and inarticulated, sublimated rage,
This flesh pulped in God's hands, the saviour surgeon
Who makes and unmakes us in his own image,
These prayers of the dying in copperplate arabesques,
Fingers throttling the wheel, knuckles blanched,
Kilometres blurred in the rushing of seconds,
Jaw clenched, tongue dry: Ich bin, Ich bin,
Ich bin uber alles, a swastika tattoo
Where the heart used to be, a gold plate tie pin
Pinning back black tie to daz-white shirt.
These prayers of the dead, embossed gothic initials
Tasteful coppertone, black leather Armani briefcase,
Celluloid images Rorsach strobed on retina
Steroid stimulants insidiously corroding cavernous tracks
Through marshmallow concrete into the depths of cerebellum,
Ich bin, Ich bin nichts, a swastika catherine wheel
In the sluice ducts of the sacral chakra,
Gas pedal crushed to floor, adrenalin flooding
Carburettor compressing explosions of thin black blood,
The porn mag in the briefcase bulging
Airbrushed gloss tits and cunt passively waiting,
Tarmacadam sweeping by in rainwet streak,
God's semen fertilising the sleeping earth,
Ich bin, Ich bin alles, tomorrow belongs to whom?
L.C.D. blinks on and off, a bland heartbeat,
Time passing between service stations and junctions,
Cutting up some old fart hogging the fast lane,
Raging with the raw jazz blood thumping amphetamine,
Tongue desert dry, swallowing motorway dust,
Adam's apple pumping like a sheared piston,
Paradise forgotten, the fruit rotten and maggot ridden,
Speeding on, into the grey wet sunset,
From city to city
And coast to coast,
A zeitgeist refugee,
A formless, unholy ghost.

THE APPLE EATER

I am falling into your cold glossy arms,
In love with your loveless eyes,
In awe of your plastic passion:
A palsied fool, tumbling down
Into empty wells of empty promise,
Into the deep soulless abyss.

FROM THE WONDROUS BURGH OF EDEN
ANOTHER ANGEL FALLS

Ether sky on Cramond Promenade / sun sinking into cold darkness / oil black firth / carious mouth / its halitous breath stinging the eyes.

Tiredness in bones & head. The raw, filthy tiredness of chemical entropy. And the dreams & visions are too far away. Over the hills & far away. This. This. And that. Cauterized hopes. Pissing on the cathartic fire. Cramped viscera. Ureic secretion. Dyscentric megababble. A toppled tower. A burnt library. A pile of words. This high! This. This. This & that. Sun sinking beyond dear green place. Saturated silhouette. Irreverant reverie. Penumbraic memorababble. A severing of tongues: dissection of brains. A hundred tribes trampling down the green grass. Shards. Slivers. The shattering of the glorified glass cow. The almighty lord, well displeased. The residents, diseased. A thousand plagues upon their heads. A thousand curses on the turncoat renegade.

Tap once, tap twice. There's no place like home.

Acid tripping thru' Pilton Paradise. Skyscrapers scraping the sky. Track marks down gangrenous veins. Empty Eldorado. Thunderbirds are go. The tough get going. Junked out on the briny Forth. Vultures circling high above, cutting arcs of stark black rainbow. Unclean rain silting up the river. The river running past Eve & Adam. A river of melted black macadam.

Shock sore eyes. Dirty dishes piled high. This high! In my sink of damaged dreams. Twenty dead salmon, soaked in rich deep crimson blood, thrashing angrily in stainless steel captivity: staring with accusing eyes.

This fish never swam. This tree never grew. This bell never rang. This puir wee chookie bird never flew.

The waters wash over. Saline detergent. I emerge, less than clean. Sun sinks down, red & blistered, west of destiny. Beyond the queen's ferry. Vagina Rex. God save her. And on, on into the sallow, slipping, listless, lapping unfrothed waters. Spume spewing from unfine oil refineries.

I dip my spent wick. This. That. This & that. This clock goes 'tic toc'. The sun unwinds, turns back, turns black; and another angel falls.

MA DURGA'S LAMENT

All my lost children are drowning:
Time is a river
And the television is violent,
Full of broken promises.

The moon has fallen into the gutter;
And even the flowers are laughing,
Hysterical,
Brittle as my broken children.

3: Dragnet

RED DREAMS AND RAZORBLADES

Imagine.

I see the hero-figure / hear the wind on the window / feel it cold on my feet / I'm frightened / on my own again.

Christmas! Christ was born on the cross! Everywhere, these grey, sick, evil faces – grotesque masks – down every street you walk. "Where," I ask, "is the salvation?" I've asked this question so many times, it reverberates in my skin, in the sky, in the walls of this room: an unholy *AUM*. Create, maintain, destroy. This pattern repeats, ad infinitum, but why?

Once, I thought I touched God… but it may just have been psilocybe psychosis, or touching into someone else's dreams.

The ghoststeps and the lullabyebyes are in my bone soul: their voices… like the dribbling away of sand. Out in the hall, there's something weird/ wired… and there is no connection to my body, which is pulsing, on its own. And now, I'm coasting over the city skyline; and far down below, scrabbled in the corner of a room, a small boy crying.

I am numb, sucked in by flashes of astral blue. Abraxas is crouched over me, whispering pictures into my eyes: my father's thunderface; my mother and her sweet razor.

Abraxas touches me. His hand inscribes a pentacle on my forehead: stabs ice into my solar plexus. I burn. I melt. I die a little.

The mist plays on my tongue. I'm hungry. I must have more.

I suck heavy on a cigarette / drown down the feeling again / struggle to obliterate the silence / but I falter / and the silence turns against me.

And an unseen hand writes on the sheeted mirror: RED DREAMS AND RAZORBLADES. Red dreams: the mess that razors made.

Ha! I cut myself from me in the name of freedom and ended up chained and bound.

These ribbons round my wrist cut and burn and twist, but I am numb. I feel nothing.

I want to run away, become a machine: I'm sick of stumbling.
  I shall sleep no more. I am a beggar on midnight street.
  See these hands? They are blue-white, bloodless lard. I hold them
out: my eyes, pleading.
  See these rib bones protruding? I am hungry. No-one will feed me.

I don't want death. I don't want rebirth. I want Brahman: perfection,
freedom and love.
All I've got is embarrassment & cold draughts: chains and masturbation.

I want flight. Perfect flight.

SONGS ARE LIKE TATTOOS

tHIS night / i am strung up as two CATs on heat / up the wALLs & halfway across the ceiling / REELING / three in tHE fucked up MORNING / screaming (silently, in the silent city).

   dreams

      have

         gone

            to

               sleep.

                  and a mILLion teleVISION sets sit cOLDly, lonely, in forgotten corners / and i sit, cold, alone, in the blue, untalking light / wishing wishes & pissing into the hurricane.

Out there / in the dARKness / another window BLAZES out tungsten sorrow / high frequency tension / a fellow sufferer, reviling against mORPHEUS's caress for free in the morning, dark madness.

But this is not the Chelsea Hotel / Joni Mitchell is not at her piano, playing 'Blue'.

NOT STILLBIRTH NOT REBIRTH

Untouchable night. Rainbows riven & forged in rusted iron. Sweet Christ! To be born into this! The light mutates into splintering silence.

Post-modern. A crown of fibre optic & razorwire. Concrete cross on a wasteland.

Dreams gear down into underdrive & the city skyline is blunted by fathom deep cloud. River runs past Eve & Adam. Into sad mire & bogland. Here, in this untactile, tactful, unplaceable place, every face is the mother-smothered mask of a solicitor, cast in a grimace of distaste.

Here, there's no explosion of laughter, no riot of colour: only the supped cup of numbness & quiet disquiet. The river runs like a slag silted tearduct: lustless & lacklustre. The television articulates our fears & lack of hope: now that paradise has been lost; and poor wee Alice has been sucked out of the looking glass.

WHITE HAND

My china white
Horsesmack hand
Writhes still
In the moonlight.
Silver winged
Fingers glow
Translucent.

Little buds of blood
Grow & bloom
& flourish:
Florid scars
Decay in parabola;
A half-life
Half-cock
Entropy.
My cup
Overfloweth.

BLACK NIGHT

Bones saturated in darkness,
Degenerating,
A faint trail of decay,
Ephemeral dust
Of half life:
A ghost voice calls.

Echoes, half way up
Or half way down
This mountain.

Mother, the napalm is burning up
Inside my dead head
And all the angels are coming
To tuck me up in bed.

I dream these echoes,
Treading dead wood water,
Misty & forgetting.

Mother is in the flower garden
Drinking pink gin, she stares
Dead eyed at a dead world.
She is dead for all the world
To see.

OPIUM HAIKUS

#1

Drugged on their death beds
They worship the puppet king
Chanting for God's blood.

#2

Junk head stares vacant
Black crater eyes reflecting
The black void of sky.

NIGHT HAIKUS

#1
Pregnant moon, chill night
Clouds scratched across a clear sky
Stream's voice in debate.

#2
The stark moon weeps soft
Luminescent, fathomless
Tears of starless loch.

LIVED AS TIME EMITS A DEVIL

The sand sinks you under:
The moon ages,
But does the mirror?

You eat sick dinner
And swallow bitter
The silver slivers.

Quietly flows the river now,
Carrying little boats
Out to sea.

The television violates
Clear space, breaking
The bird in your heart.

4: Eyes That Were Pearls

SHE HOLDS HERSELF SO TIGHT
THE SKIN TURNS WHITE

she holds herself so tight the skin turns white/ the skin so tight, she curls/ an embryo form/ a curve of laughter behind mirrors/ she agonises her agonies/ washes herself in moonlight/ her body bleached / curled up pale upon the rocks/ a whisper of finger, curled on her breast.

her hair is black, oil black/ witch's hair, her hair/ her cunt hair is a finger/ cool blue finger/ drawn with lipstick licks/ her eyes are black/ black as jasmine oil/ black as inside out mirrors.

her eyes are black as a jazz song/ her skin as white as the crone moon/ inside her, the moon is an ocean.

inside her, the baby seed grows/ she vomits/ collapses in a heap of her vomit.

the cigarette burns down/ his hand is motionless, curled round his metal penis.

the ocean does not wash her body smell/ does not wash away the jasmine, sweat and come/ it breaks her body on sharp white rocks.

her laugh is a thousand splinters.

white rocks, white body, white moon/ the blue sky is too blue/ it hurts the eyes/ too blue, like the waters breaking on her shoreline.
    she dreams that she's an island.

the sky is too blue/ the grass is too green/ too green, like the too green snake which slithers on its belly thru' the too green grass.

the trees are black/ just right/ black, like her witch's hair/ the trees reach up and reach up.

she holds herself tight/ her skin, white/ tight/ taut/ an embryo form curving/ carved from mirror.
her belly is ripe, but the milk is sour.

•

her glass gown was too long, too tight/ she should have danced all night.
oh baby, oh baby, please!/ his voice teased her clothes to splinters.

•

her black hair dangles loose/ untied of its rainbow ribbons/ black hair against white skin/ lipstick lips painted on a bloodless face.

cunt red/ the lipstick kisses on his brass torso/ "oh baby baby please"/ cunt juice acid on his brass cock/ glass splinters in his hand/ brass/ glass/ fragments of carriage clock/ a chronological mockery.

chronos: the god who sucks the soul.

•

the ballroom is empty/ masks & broken glass on the polished floor/ the caretaker sweeping up/ his uniform, blacker than the night.

she is eggshell/ laughing/ washed up/ white/ her hair, black as bitumen/ reeking of jasmine oil.
he is brass, skeletal/ robed in black/ black as krisstallnacht.
she is oval glass/ splintering/ fragmenting to the dead moon's call.
he stretches out his metal fingers/ they are all for the grabbing/ greedy baby/ his only wish: impregnation.

•

oh baby baby please/ the black semen saturating the milky egg/ his naked brass body, suddenly limpid/ the acid seed in her belly/ fragments of metal & glass scattered across the polished wood floor/ luminous brass/ opaque glass.

he sings in his sleep/ oh baby baby, I'm begging you please.
    she listens to the moon and the waves in her belly.
    she cries a river of glass and jasmine oil.

in her palm/ a sliver of glass/ the wound, a cunt/ a stigmata/ a reminder: there is no joy that cannot be broken.
    for every cocktail there is a crucifixion.

•

she is white, cold, alone/ the baby grows inside her/ a monstruous incubus, sucking the life out of her.
    she is eggshell bits, splinters of glass, specks of moonlight/ all wrapped up in dead white skin.

the caretaker sweeps her up/ into his plastic bag/ black/ black as the devil's seed/ he sweeps her up with all the weekend's detritus/ bottles, cans, ciga-rette packets, condoms & paper hankies/ lipstick containers, masks and fragments of brass & glass.
    he pushes his brush languidly thru' all the trash/ whistling his favourite pop song/ oh baby, oh baby please/ I'll get down on my knees...

she curls up in a thousand splinters/ curls up in the rubbish of a thousand dreams/ she only wanted to dance/ she only wanted to dance.
    the crone moon calls her/ calls the waves in her belly/ she curls up/ cramps/ the skin ripples/ taut/ tortured/ impaled/ she holds herself/ tight/ she holds herself so tight the skin turns white.

STALEMATE

The evil king is
Dead of soul
& black of night:
A swastika tattoo
Where the heart
Used to be.
He bows down
& worships
His shipwrecked mind.

ALONE AND IN TATTERS

The moon curls in upon itself,
Enfolding the light,
Tight in her barren belly.
The telly flickers,
Icy white and bright blue,
Casts shadows of my skeletal frame
Onto the blank walls of this bedsit room.

Alone then, am I,
Gazing beyond city chimney stacks
At the darkening dome of sky,
Shivering
In the misty misery of solitude:
All the bridges are painted over now,
My fields are flooded with salt rain
And the cows are no longer milking.

HARBOUR OF STILL WATERS

If in this doll's house ever I scream out
I am gagged with marshmallow clouds
And made to smile.

I am bright light,
Golden violet,
A stream of snowmelt,
My head filled with rainbows.

Swallows, slow motion,
Flit over marigold fields
And father grins into the fireplace,
Whisky hazed and mellowed.

Bruised have paled to blush
And broken cups have been swept up:
Everything is tidy now.

I am happy,
Happier than I ever thought I could be:
In this bubble no trouble can touch me.

I am safe:
Away from the pulsebeat,
The throb and drone
Of clashing machinery.

Safe and sound:
It is always summer now in my dreams.

NIGHT FOLLOWS DAY FOLLOWS NIGHT
FOLLOWS DAY FOLLOWS...

Isn't it good that everything follows the pattern?
That we are snug and secure in our little nest egg:
That we've got computers and duties and securities;
And insurance policies too.

Isn't it good that we've got this far?

Isn't it good that night follows day and day follows night?

And haven't we got far? We've got names for the atoms
And names for the stars.

Isn't it good we've dispensed with superstition
For the sweet vision of rationality: the ice cream dream
Of consumption? I mean, every man must have a house.
Every man must have a car.

Night follows day without a nightmare it seems.

Yes, we've got drugs that rub out the bad dreams.
Everything is, just as it seems:
Everybody's happy nowadays.

THE SYLKIE BOY

Whispering. Wishing. With the water washing over. Swish swish.
I wish, I wish. And him limp, listless. Lying lumpen and leaden; deadened,
decaying.

No, not even praying: not anymore.

An ocean for a wishing well. White sands yellowing in the foam. And
the water comfortably warm: of woman, of womb. Sucking and sliding.
Creeping up and sifting away.

And his head muggy with words and wishes. Fishes and kisses.
Sandcastle and sirens singing. The sun beating down.

And somewhere distant someone laughing.

The water licking his back with its clammy tongue.
The wind carrying soft syllables. I wish, I wish.
And his feet bobbing in the water.

And him tasting, not tasting, the water in his mouth.
The briny effluence, analgesic and addictive:
Drinking it into his lungs.

Now floating so sweetly, under the water, with the fishes.
Laughter and singing, undulating.
Heady as mulled wine
Or the first kiss of a cigarette.

Drifting. Twisting with the eddies. Not feeling. Not seeing. Not waving.
Not caring. No.

Not even praying.

Not anymore.

AUTUMN IN FLORENCE

In the grape garden,
Wistful dreaming,
A sallow content settles,
Musty as Amaretto.

The men play cards,
Watch television,
Their faces wrinkled,
Brown as walnuts.

The breeze scatters
Russet leaves,
Blackbirds rain down
Grapes from heaven.

The stromclouds gather,
Heavily laden:
Thunder rumbles close,
Dark as an omen.

A MINOR RETURN

Soft, wet flesh night. A christening.
Seminal birthpangs in bed of apple
eating dreams. Cunt taste. Clitoral
tang. Fading into morning. Strewn
sheets. Half unpacked bags. Settled.
Unsettled. A sack of memories and a
big stirring spoon. Expectations.
Beyond the here & now. Not sleeping.
Sun rising. Acid colourless light.
The walls conspire to breathe. And
I feel breathless, restless; listening
to the dull beating heart of this
sleeping, strange, too familiar city.

WAITING FOR WINTER

I look at you & you look at me:
Murky faced reflection;
Turning, twisting grey,
Dreaming of faraway.
Timeless, listless, frozen:
Emptied out into the ocean.

We are faraway, miles away:
Hands outstretched,
Not touching.

5: Catharsis

IN A HOUSE OF FIRE

Away from the scorched sky
In the entrails of this cave
Even the darkness is red
Jewels fade into bloodless flowers
And the strange stench
Of fathom-deep places and fear.

Tensing a calloused hand
The senses untouched
Tongue cleft and parched
Utters cursed penitence
For a cloudburst.

The acrid soil, I spill
The split seed tumbles yellow
Brittle dust scratches
Retinal fireflashes
Scours the sad skin
Withering and vacant.

APPLE MAGGOTS

I shall purge myself,
Scour my insides
With caustic fire,
Tear the hair
From my head;
And bleeding,
Walk naked
Thru' the jeering
Heaving mass.

VALIUM SUNSET

Rainbows & spindrift. The clouds roll in.
Headshroud. I roll another decadent cigarette
And head for the doortsep of wheeling whirling
chaffinches. Press siren bells into my skull.
I try to teach them to sing. Tame & tune.
Touch the big noise of hallucination. Sweating
in the sterile sitting room. Blue-grey carpet.
Brown sofa & chairs. Headpulse. Taste of
stodge on the tongue. The lover driftdreams
in glossy magazine. I take scissors and mutilate
obscure truths, torn and cut, from the wildest,
crudest, most alluring lies. The lipstick
blowjob. Power make up. Powder, pigment &
whalefat. Paint cuntlips over my eyes and
am sublimely blind. Crawling over cesspits
in the flickering television light. Dead soul.
Crater eyed lust. Sweet bird of death. Rainbow
knotted round my throat. Listlessly lying
on the rim of the black lipped pit. Abraxas
wants me to fly, but won't lend me his wings.

TO BE BURNING

Day of thunder,
Thor's domain:
I am full of fire,
Dreams of raw bone.

Waking screaming,
I fly swallow tailed
Thru' locked wards:
Shaking cobwebs
And stained linen;
Naked into
The thrashing wind.

The sea women haunt me
With suicidal melodies:
Songs of the crone moon
Echo in their womb blood.

The frost lays barren
My grape garden,
Grips it in iron jaws.
The sun whispers
Promises of abundance
And purification.

I cannot stand
This tenderness:
It unloops me.

I leap up
And kiss the clouds,
Drink the burning waters,
Surrender,
Wave a white flag,
Unseen
In the white wastes
Of frozen night.

AWAITING THE STORM

I skulk away from the sky,
Hide under a rock shelter,
Look out
Over the stagnant pools,
Wait
For the rain to come.

And, you know,
I never thought
It would happen like this:
Those old sylvan warriors
Are waiting for me,
Round the corner.

They have no weapons,
Only red brittle faces
With half-smiles
And words
Which I barely understand.

PRE-BIRTH

A pissing spring. Bitter evening.
February. The cruellest month.
Dry desperation. I want, I want.
I want to rip bloody strips
From the hand that thinks it feeds.

The sky cracks open, orange flame:
A premonition. neon spewed forth
Over bleak terrain. Arid piss.
Angry bile in constricted throat.
I want, I need.
I want to tear my head off
& throw it in the pissing river.

LOTUS

Kissing two in the morning
With some foreign urgency
In my blood,
As if I were to crack
The stone silence of dawn
And draw out
A thousand petalled flower.

THE FIRST TRUMPET

Dawn cracks open
The last of days,
The Ganga flows
Apocalyptic
Past funeral pyres,
Thru' crumbling towns.

The lovers burn
Umbilical threads,
Burst stars
And empty bottles
In sleeping halls.

THE LAST LAUGH

Hiding in the shrubbery
Palms down, eyes closed
Waiting for the hunting horse,
White & crystal
& salt mane sweeping
& witch burning eyes.
   Waiting for the cold blood
Knife in the guts
& twist, twist twice
& then
Just nothing –
Empty
Ethereal.
   Waiting & wanting
Craving the cut
& thrust;
The thunder,
The dying sigh,
The scream
& the silence.
   Waiting behind the leaves,
Leaving behind the dreams,
Dreaming behind the mask. She says:
"I got the last laugh –
I got the last laugh on you."

6: Suffering A Sea Change

REBIRTH

In the dark crimson secret cellar I crawl.
A fistful of miseries. Knees crammed into
jawbone. Simulation of stillbirth rage.
Not gently into that good night. Old man
of harrowed brow & grinding incisors.

These splintered teeth. The soft fat torn
from fetid meat. Cold granite chewed to pulp.

Oh! I hear no skylark sing. In death I need
no nourishment. No joyous spring. No fountain.
No snow-capped, clear-aired mountain. I am what
I eat. Rotten meat.

Behind this ragged cuntflap I wait, a pale saint,
for judgement.

Incarnate. In babywet flesh, new pink hope &
forgetting. A recycle of milky tit, girning &
bedwetting. A bloodletting. My mammary mammy
screams out: it's coming, it's coming. I kick
out & bite my tiny fists. Raging out of that
dark good night. Drunk on the somnolent river
of no returning. Pushed. Secreted. A thunder
storm of scalding hot, damp, loving muscle.

Oh! My watery expanded mother cries: a boy.
No joy. I peer in tear-smeared terror at the
too bright, too white world. Blur of monstrous
purple faces. Tinnitus scouring of ears.
I roar. Not going gently to that good light.
Unintelligible: in fear, loathing & smacked
arse pain. My first breath: oh fuck, not again!

RAINBOW THUNDER

MOURNFUL HEAD. MORNING HEAD. RAINBOW BLISTERS ON YR FINGERS. Stretch up to heaven and yawn a big yawn into the wild blue window. Snatched back yr scratched bag. Big sexy grin as you throw yrself out of the covers. All period blood & sperm smell wafting up to nicotine nostrils. Rainbows & dreams all over yr eyes. You were Kerouac last night, jumping a freight train across the mid-west, irony on yr face & meat in yr belly. You leapt across the quantum and over the moon. Drift dreaming beyond the precipice. You lift. You live. Talking in tongues. Raving like a fucking madman. Tic talking. You chuck yr watch over the Talahatchy River, train thumping by, obliterating the sharp shattering cacophony of watchspring & glass. Kali tells you it will thunder, but you don't know. Always there is that pressure in yr head. The sound of sirens, bells & screams. A tumour of tension & dreams; and always you are running like fuck, running away. A murder of blue black crows in your hair. Freedom. Freedom to feed yr dream. TINNITUS HEAD. DREAMING HEAD. I AM MR RAINBOW. I AM THAT BIG.

LAMENT FOR CROW

If we could fill it
        up
    the black void
    in my bleak
        blackened heart,
soot blasted
glasgow dreaming
blue eyed boy.

Gorse & heather
Wind blows thru'
Leaking arteries.

Blood.
Black bile.

I love you,
but I've forgotten yr name.
Hold me forever
in yr sweet
sweat stained
shadow.

Ghost moon
brooding.
Silhouette of black bird.

I dreamed of this.

BIRTH

I struggle with you
Words of stone
Thru' the cuntwound
Of type bruised
Finger flesh.

Every story, every poem:
A labour,
A fiery birth.
My sweet babies.

Sweet sticky babies,
Filthy
& beautiful
In the blood
& heat
& joy
of orgasm
& afterbirth.

BIKE

Boy with earring
(gold skull) laughing,
swinging thru' the streets,
too happy
for commuters,
faceless buildings,
computers.

He could have ended up
dead in a back alley,
but he always said
he'd rather have a bike,
any day.

DREAM ECLIPSES REALITY

Yesterday I painted
Great big happy faces
On all the skyscrapers
In the Gorbals...
And what if skyscrapers
Really did scrape
The sky?
I would attach paintbrushes
Dripping with rainbow colours
To their radio masts
And lightning conductors.

PHAEDRUS

I imagine my father is phaedrus
And one day he will return
With paint in his eyes
And emeralds instead of false teeth.

TINDERSTICKS

Sometimes we touch in the deepest place:
It is not that blue and red make purple,
But that colour, freed of itself,
Can merge with the light.

CLOSING THE DOOR

Opening the coffin lid, Candy
Your marbled clotted face
Appalled me
And your black cratered eyes
Stared so,
Stilling the blood
For a moment
There.

Aye, but we buried you, Candy
In Paris
In the cemetery
Where the hippies sat
Smashed out
And downcast
By the lizard king's
Gravestone.

And they played guitars, Candy
Sweet rhythmic pulses
We could have
Danced away the night to,
But you were dead, Candy
And I had to dance
Alone.